D1709645

NATURAL DISASTERS

Sinkholes

by Rebecca Pettiford

BELLWETHER MEDIA • MINNEAPOLIS, MN

Note to Librarians, Teachers, and Parents:

Blastoff! Readers are carefully developed by literacy experts and combine standards-based content with developmentally appropriate text.

Level 1 provides the most support through repetition of high-frequency words, light text, predictable sentence patterns, and strong visual support.

Level 2 offers early readers a bit more challenge through varied simple sentences, increased text load, and less repetition of high-frequency words.

Level 3 advances early-fluent readers toward fluency through increased text and concept load, less reliance on visuals, longer sentences, and more literary language.

Level 4 builds reading stamina by providing more text per page, increased use of punctuation, greater variation in sentence patterns, and increasingly challenging vocabulary.

Level 5 encourages children to move from "learning to read" to "reading to learn" by providing even more text, varied writing styles, and less familiar topics.

Whichever book is right for your reader, Blastoff! Readers are the perfect books to build confidence and encourage a love of reading that will last a lifetime!

This edition first published in 2020 by Bellwether Media, Inc.

No part of this publication may be reproduced in whole or in part without written permission of the publisher. For information regarding permission, write to Bellwether Media, Inc., Attention: Permissions Department, 6012 Blue Circle Drive, Minnetonka, MN 55343.

Library of Congress Cataloging-in-Publication Data

Names: Pettiford, Rebecca, author.
Title: Sinkholes / by Rebecca Pettiford.
Description: Minneapolis : Bellwether Media, 2020. | Series: Blastoff! readers. Natural disasters | Includes bibliographical references and index. | Audience: Ages 5-8 | Audience: Grades 2-3 | Summary: ""Simple text and full-color photography introduce beginning readers to sinkholes. Developed by literacy experts for students in kindergarten through third grade"-Provided by publisher"-- Provided by publisher.
Identifiers: LCCN 2019028702 (print) | LCCN 2019028703 (ebook) | ISBN 9781644871539 (library binding) | ISBN 9781618918291 (ebook)
Subjects: LCSH: Sinkholes--Juvenile literature.
Classification: LCC GB609.2 .P47 2020 (print) | LCC GB609.2 (ebook) | DDC 551.4/7--dc23
LC record available at https://lccn.loc.gov/2019028702
LC ebook record available at https://lccn.loc.gov/2019028703

Text copyright © 2020 by Bellwether Media, Inc. BLASTOFF! READERS and associated logos are trademarks and/or registered trademarks of Bellwether Media, Inc.

Editor: Rebecca Sabelko   Designer: Josh Brink

Printed in the United States of America, North Mankato, MN

Table of **Contents**

What Are Sinkholes?

sinkhole

Sinkholes are holes in the ground. Some are small. Others can be thousands of feet deep! Sinkholes may grow slowly. Some **collapse** suddenly.

They happen where rock below the ground's surface is weak.

Sinkhole Areas

N
W — E
S

common sinkhole areas
in the United States =

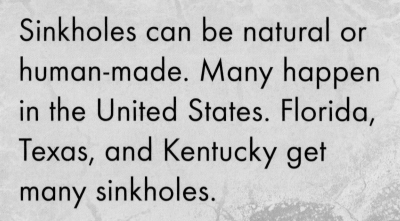

Sinkholes can be natural or human-made. Many happen in the United States. Florida, Texas, and Kentucky get many sinkholes.

sinkhole in Florida

sinkhole in Russia

But they can happen all over the world!

Water **erosion** causes
natural sinkholes. Water
mixes with **carbon dioxide**.
It becomes **acidic**.

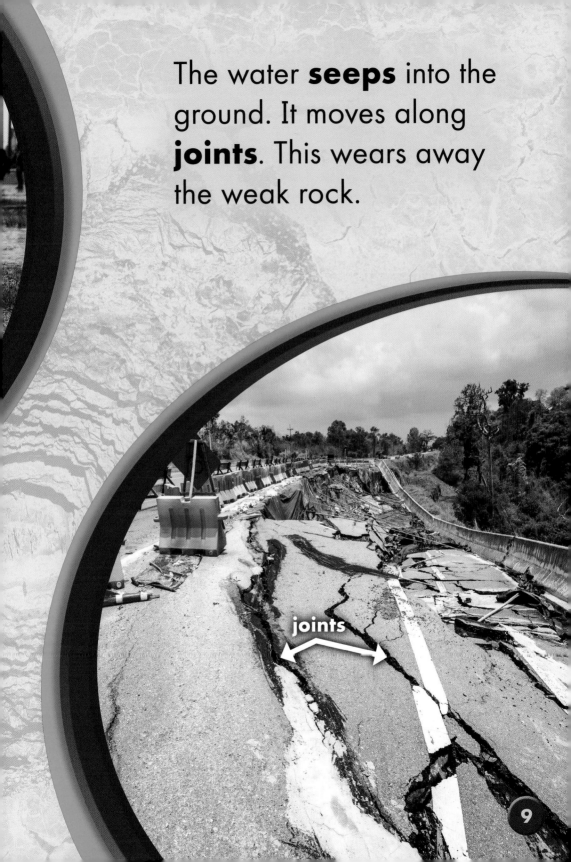

The water **seeps** into the ground. It moves along **joints**. This wears away the weak rock.

joints

The joints get bigger as the rock wears away. They become unstable. **Cavities** form near the surface of the ground. The sinkhole grows! The ground's surface weakens. Then it collapses!

How Sinkholes Form

water wears away rock

soil and rock fall

hole grows and surface weakens

surface falls

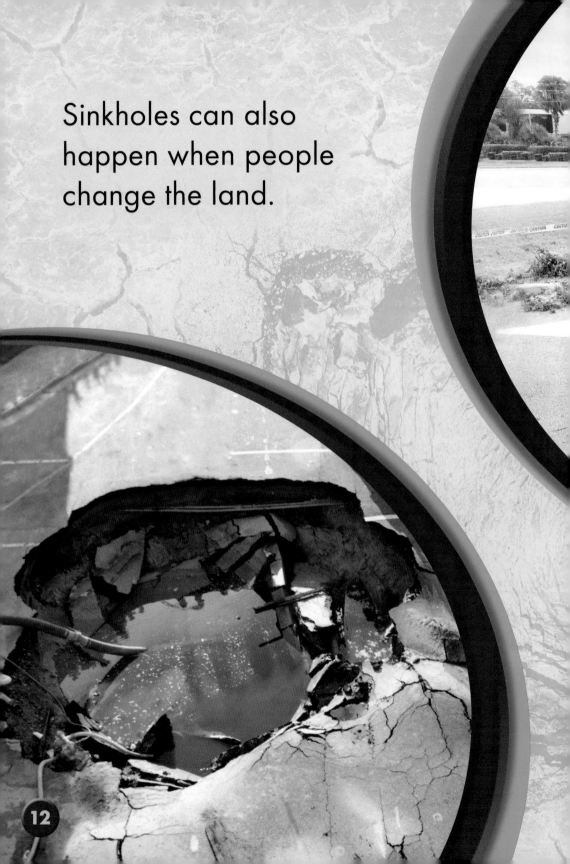

Sinkholes can also happen when people change the land.

Roads can cause water to
gather on the ground.
The water washes away
layers of rock.

Sinkhole Damage

Sinkholes can destroy roads and buildings. People can get hurt if they fall in.

Sinkholes can also **pollute** drinking water.

polluted water

15

It is not possible to stop natural sinkholes. But the number of human-made sinkholes can be lessened.

Plumbing can cause sinkholes. Keep pipes in working order. This can stop sudden holes from forming.

Sinkhole Profile

Name: 2010 Guatemala City Sinkhole

Date: May 30, 2010

Location: Guatemala City, Guatemala

Cause: human and natural

Size: 65 feet (20 meters) across
300 feet (91 meters) deep

2010 Guatemala City Sinkhole

Scientists can **predict** where sinkholes may happen. They use special tools.

They can find areas on the ground that are sinking or getting weaker.

scientists searching for sinkholes

18

Florida Sinkhole Report

Danger Level	How Close to Home?
Least:	• none within 10 miles (16 kilometers)
Very low:	• 1 mile (2 kilometers) to 10 miles (16 kilometers)
Low:	• within 1 mile (2 kilometers)
Mild:	• 0.5 miles (0.8 kilometers) to 1 mile (2 kilometers)
High:	• less than 0.5 miles 0.8 kilometers)
Very high:	• close to home
Highest:	• sinkhole next to home

Sinkholes give **warning** signs. Fence posts sag. Trees bend. Windows and doors may not close well.

It is best to stay far away
from sinkholes. Standing
next to one is dangerous!

Glossary

acidic—having the qualities of acid; acid is something that can break things apart.

carbon dioxide—a gas released when animals breathe out or when fuels burn

cavities—unfilled spaces under the ground

collapse—to suddenly break apart or fall down

erosion—the slow wearing away of something

joints—broken areas or gaps in rock

plumbing—a system of pipes for supplying and carrying water

pollute—to make dirty or unusable

predict—to use information to guess what may happen

seeps—flows or passes slowly through small openings

warning—something that tells someone about possible danger

To Learn More

AT THE LIBRARY

Black, Vanessa. *Sinkholes*. Minneapolis, Minn.:
Jump!, 2017.

Squire, Ann O. *Sinkholes*. New York, N.Y.: Children's
Press, 2016.

Westcott, Jim. *Natural Disasters*. Mankato, Minn.: Black
Rabbit Books, 2018.

ON THE WEB

FACTSURFER

Factsurfer.com gives you
a safe, fun way to find
more information.

1. Go to www.factsurfer.com.

2. Enter "sinkholes" into the search box and click Q.

3. Select your book cover to see a list of related web sites.

Index

The images in this book are reproduced through the courtesy of: IrinaK, front cover (house); Istvan Csak, front cover (car); a katz, front cover (sinkhole); Konstantnin, pp. 2-3; cdsb/ AP Images, p. 4; Alexander Ryumin/ Getty Images, p. 6; Orlando Sentinel/ Getty Images, p. 7; Makarov Konstantin, p. 8; Piyawat Nandeenopparit, p. 9; Poliorketes, p. 10; John Spink/ AP Images, p. 12; Michael Warren, p. 13; McClatchy-Tribune/ Alamy, p. 14; Corbis News/ Getty Images, p. 15; muratart, p. 16; Moises Castillo/ AP Images, p. 17; Nik Taylor/ Alamy, p. 18; Caroline Del, p. 19; Neologizer, p. 20; ZUMA Press/ Alamy, p. 21.